KITTENS

KITTENS

Joyce Robins

‖ •PARRAGON• ‖

Acknowledgements

Bruce Coleman Ltd/Jane Burton jacket, pages 9, 10, 11, 13, 14, 16, 17, 21, 22, 24, 27, 29, 30, 35, 40, 42, 45, 47, 48, 50, 53, 54, 55, 57, 60, 63, 64, 65, 67, 70, 71, 72, 76; **/Fritz Prenzel** page 74; **/Hans Reinhard** pages 23, 37, 59, 75; **ZEFA** pages 6, 18, 33, 34, 39, 43, 44, 49, 58; **Sally Anne Thompson/Animal Photography** pages 68, 78.

First published in Great Britain in 1994 by
Parragon Book Service Ltd
Units 13-17, Avonbridge Trading Estate
Atlantic Road, Avonmouth
Bristol BS11 9QD

Publishing Manager: Sally Harper
Editor: Anne Crane
Design: Robert Mathias/Helen Mathias

ISBN 1 85813 876 0

Printed in Italy

Contents

CHAPTER ONE

Starting Out

Kittens are easy to love and there are few hearts that do not melt at the sight of these furry bundles tottering on tiny legs. They are also easy enough to understand because all they need at first is food, sleep and warmth. But a kitten is an embryo cat and brings with it all the mystique of thousands of years of the cat family. It may look sweet and dependent and adoring as it snuggles into the palm of your hand but its make-up is already programmed with all the natural feline assurance, courage and self-sufficiency. You can love your cat, provide for it and share your home with it for fifteen years or more, yet you may never completely understand it. The cat will give you affection, companionship and fun but only on its own terms. Rudyard Kipling, in his

FACING PAGE: Three young kittens explore the outside world for the first time.

Just So Stories, told how our ancestors tricked the horse, the cow and the dog into becoming their servants but they met their match in the cat, who tricked them into providing a saucer of warm milk and a place of honour by the fire. It would co-operate just enough to become part of the household but 'when the moon gets up and night comes, he is the cat that walks by himself.'

No one has to teach cats how to be mothers; it seems to be a natural part of their make-up. White cats have a reputation as poor carers, but this is probably because they incline to deafness, and do not hear their kittens crying for attention or squeaking with fright when they have wandered too far and need rescue, so that they appear to be ignoring or neglecting them. Feckless feline mothers do occur, but they are very much the exception. I knew of a former stray, who, having found herself a home with a loving family produced a litter of five kittens but after a fortnight decided this was far too much like hard work and left. She took up residence at a local dress shop and her owners, struggling to bring up the abandoned family, saw her from time to time, taking her ease in the sunny shop window, but they could never tempt her to come back.

Most cats do a much better job. A breeder friend says that one of her three cats, Bonnet, obviously sees motherhood as her life's work. Recently three mothers with litters were strategically placed in different rooms of the house for peace and privacy. One morning the breeder heard howls of fury and found the two downstairs nesting boxes empty. Two of her 'girls' were fighting on the stairs, presumably accusing one another of stealing kittens. In the upstairs box lay Bonnet, feet in the air, with fourteen kittens of various ages trampling over one another in a frantic effort to get at her milk. She had poached each of the kittens, one by one, carrying them upstairs to join her own family and was wearing a look of blissful satisfaction.

Lucky dip litter

Litters of kittens can contain surprises, even for the careful breeder, but the mating of a pedigree cat will be supervised with care, and the stud chosen to improve the stock and bring the kittens nearer to the standards set for the breed. If the mother's colour is too light or her tail has a kink, she will be mated with a stud that has a darker coat or an absolutely straight tail. It is a very different story for the ordinary house cat. When nature takes over she won't choose the prospective father by the length of his coat or his attractive colour, she will mate with the nearest tom or, more likely, with all the toms that happen to be available. Her owner will not know which cat has fathered the kittens, so the litter will be something of a lucky dip, their appearance governed by the pattern of genes inherited from their parents.

Colour, too, is governed by genes. Tabby, governed by what is called the 'agouti' gene, is the natural coat colour for cats. In the wild it is the best type of

FACING PAGE: *A mother suckles her kittens, which knead her flank as they feed.*

camouflage and the colour of wild cats evolved accordingly: charcoal grey for forest dwellers and sandy for the occupants of the desert. Experts believe that the modern cat is descended from the African Wild Cat, which proved its adaptability thousands of years ago by moving near to agricultural settlements to hunt for rodents, then accepting food and shelter and learning to live alongside man. Cats were certainly domesticated by about 3000 BC, for they appear in the wall paintings of the tombs of Ancient Egypt, often sitting under a woman's chair as a symbol of fertility. These were tabbies with faint markings and it was probably only when they were imported to Europe and mated with the European Wild Cat that they developed the more definite markings we see today.

Geneticists explain that all modern cats are tabbies underneath, but that some genes overlay the effect of others, so that a solid colour masks the tabby pattern. If that seems difficult to believe, notice how many kittens are born with faint tabby markings that disappear as they mature. The first variation on the tabby colouring was probably black, a mutation that blots out tabby banding and which is found

among the big cats. Later this was diluted to colours like brown, chocolate and blue. The agouti gene is dominant to the non-agouti gene, so if a tabby and a black cat mate, the kittens are likely to be tabby. If a black cat mates with a chocolate cat, however, the kittens will be black. White, too, is a winner amongst genes; the white gene also produces blue eyes and a weakness in the structure of the ear, which inclines towards deafness. White cats with yellow eyes are less likely to be deaf and if one eye is blue and the other yellow, the cat may be deaf in one ear only, on the side of the blue eye.

The fertile time

There is a story about a little old lady, who was convinced that her Burmese female, scarcely out of kittenhood, was about to experience a virgin birth. She protested that the cat had never been outside and yes, there was a tom cat in the house, but they were brother and sister, so he could not possibly have done the deed. Cats are unlikely to take any notice of the moral taboos of humans and some of them are sexually mature at a very early age. Most females begin 'call-

FACING PAGE: *A tortoiseshell cat considers the possibilities of a goldfish pond.*

ABOVE: *Young cats are full of curiosity about the world around them.*

ing' for the first time at between seven and twelve months but quite a number will call at five months and with the precocious Siamese and Burmese, it can be even earlier.

The female shows no interest in mating when she is not 'on heat' (in oestrus) and will soon dispatch a tom that gets too interested at the wrong time. Wild cats have one or two periods of oestrus between spring and summer, so that their offspring will be born in the warmer weather, when plenty of food is available. Domestic cats have a longer breeding season, but the heat cycles are still related to climate. In the northern hemisphere the breeding season runs from January to September, peaking between February and May and again in July and August. In the southern hemisphere it runs from July to March, peaking between August and October and again in December and January. Cats kept indoors, with central heating and artificial light, may have periods of oestrus all year round.

Once oestrus begins, the cat may become hyperactive. If she is not allowed out to find a mate she will rub herself round her owner's legs, furniture and roll sensuously on the carpet. A docile cat may display bad temper and a cat that never shows the slightest interest in outdoors will search frantically for any method of escape. She will visit the litter tray more frequently than usual and may even begin to spray, because she now excretes pheromones, which give off messages that she is available for mating. All this is punctuated by a full-throated howling, designed to attract every male within hearing range. Oestrus usually lasts for five or six days and will begin all over again a couple of weeks later if she is not mated.

The courting

A free-roaming female in oestrus will soon collect a court of suitors that will follow her around, chase her if she runs away or gather below if she takes a high perch to look them over; this courting time can go on for hours. There is usually a lot of caterwauling but the males are seldom aggressive towards one another. Though the males may be anxious for action, it is the female that chooses her partners and the time for mating. Once she has chosen the first suitor she will mate with a number of different toms and

it is this behaviour that led to female cats being called queens from the old English word quean, meaning hussy. In fact, her promiscuous behaviour is probably a survival mechanism to make sure of pregnancy, for her eggs are only released after the first mating takes place. When she is ready, the female will crouch down with her rump raised and her tail held to one side. Owners find that when they stroke the back of a cat in oestrus she will automatically take up this position.

A pedigree cat will have her mating planned in a much more decorous manner. She is normally taken to the home of the stud male, rather than the other way round, as he is the one that needs to feel secure and confident in order to perform. The two cats will be housed separately but close together for the first day or so, so that they can get used to one another. Once the first mating has taken place, the female will stay for two or three days so that there can be further matings.

LEFT: *This Abyssinian mother keeps careful watch over her two-week-old kitten.*

LEFT: *Even at seven days of age, a kitten can raise an indignant growl if it senses an intruder nearby.*

Mother-to-be

Most feline mothers-to-be seem very calm and relaxed. The pregnancy usually lasts about nine weeks. After three and a half weeks, ultrasound can detect the foetal heartbeat, and after four or five weeks her tummy will begin to enlarge. At six weeks X-rays can detect the skeletal outlines of the kittens; a few days later they will start moving and the mother reacts by rolling and stretching, and begins to look for a safe quiet spot to nest. Most owners go to a lot of trouble to provide a warm, comfortable kittening box but the cat may well decide that she prefers one of the family's beds or the laundry basket. One friend provided not one, but three well-lined boxes in various choice spots, but when the crucial moment came her cat chose the vegetable rack.

When the first stage of labour begins one cat may become quite agitated. Another may sit peacefully purring and kneading with her paws, quietly waiting. This stage lasts for several hours and when the second stage begins, the cat will settle into her nest. Some cats need complete privacy, others make it quite clear that they want their owners with them by mewing and taking a few steps towards the nest, then coming back if the owner is not following, just as they lead the way to the kitchen when in urgent need of a meal.

As contractions begin in earnest, the cat will lie on her side, perhaps bracing her hind legs on the side of the box. This stage is usually short, with the first kitten arriving, neatly parcelled within its sac of membranes, in thirty minutes or so. The others may come quickly, so that the whole delivery lasts only an hour, or the mother may take long rests between each birth. I came across one female that produced four kittens one after another, then lay back for twenty-four hours before starting labour all over again, producing a fifth, large, robust kitten.

As each kitten is born, the mother gives it a vigorous licking to remove the membranes and she also deals with the cord and the afterbirth, doing the right thing by instinct. If there is another female cat in the house, she may join in the proceedings and act as a 'midwife', helping to clean up the kittens or even biting the cord. Once all the kittens have been born, the mother will clean herself up then curl round them so that they can begin to

ABOVE: *After suckling, this two-week-old kitten falls into a contented sleep.*

in proteins and minerals and with anti-bodies that provide the kittens with protection from disease for the first three months of its life, giving them a chance to build own resistance.

The new family

After the delivery, the mother needs about twelve hours' rest. For the first couple of days, she is reluctant to leave the kittens for a minute, even for a visit to the litter tray. The kittens do nothing but sleep and feed and she cares for them devotedly, working hard to keep them meticulously clean, paying particular attention to their rear ends to stimulate them to empty themselves, for they will not excrete spontaneously until they are about three weeks old. For the next few weeks her body produces prolactin, which stimulates milk production. In the rare case that kittens do not suckle, the prolactin level drops sharply and within one or two weeks, long before the kittens can fend for themselves, she will be on heat again.

Siamese are the most precocious of kittens, opening their eyes by the second or third day, while Persians and Shorthairs

suckle. At first the kittens may nurse almost continuously for eight hours at a time. By the second or third day, each kitten will have decided on a particular teat; after that they seldom change places. Kittens are born both blind and deaf, Persians and Shorthairs weighing about 114 g (4 oz) and Siamese as little as 57 g (2 oz). In the first twenty-four hours they often do not put on weight and may even lose a little but within seven days a healthy kitten will have doubled its birth weight. During the first days the mother's milk contains colostrum, a substance rich can take well over a week. In most cases the eyelids begin to part gradually, so that at first the eyes appear as slits, but sometimes one eye will open before the other. Females tend to open their eyes before males of the same litter, and if the nesting box is in a dark spot the kittens will open their eyes sooner than those exposed to normal light. Once they can see, though they still cannot stand, the kittens will start pulling themselves around on their stomachs, their feet paddling on either side. The mother is always ready to hook them back into the family circle if they wriggle too far away.

Many owners have reared orphaned or abandoned kittens on the bottle, giving them two-hourly feeds day and night. Caring for such a kitten is a delicate business because without the colostrum from its mother's milk, it will be far more vulnerable to infection. Naturally enough, a hand-reared kitten will grow up to be attached to humans and makes a very affectionate pet, but its progress will be slower than a kitten brought up in the hurly-burly of the litter, where they soon learn to compete and hold their own. If a foster mother (a cat that has just produced a litter) is available she will proba-

bly feed the orphan without fuss. Several experiments have demonstrated that cats cannot count and if the extra infant arrives early enough, she will usually take to it. New mothers seem to be so devoted to any helpless little creatures, and reports and pictures of cats with unusual families come from all over the world. A French cat called Duchesse, who had lost her litter soon after birth, happily mothered nine baby rabbits; a Danish cat fostered two squirrels and a German cat raised no objection when three hedgehogs joined her own kittens.

ABOVE: *At one day old, this ginger kitten can pull himself along and squeak but he cannot yet raise his head.*

17

CHAPTER TWO

Growing Up

FACING PAGE: At a very early age, kittens develop confidence and their individual personalities start to show.

Rearing kittens is entirely the mother's job. Even in feral cat colonies, where all the cats involved live together, toms take no interest in the female once mating has taken place, and they have nothing at all to do with the litter, offering neither food nor protection.

If the toms do come near the kittens they tread very warily, probably fearing the mother's wrath, and if a bold kitten comes forward to investigate the stranger, the tom will tap it gently away with its paw, then disappear speedily. Well-meaning owners have been known to bring in next door's tom to admire his fine offspring, as though arranging a visit to a maternity ward. This is always a disaster: the tom is bewildered by these strange little creatures, never dreaming they have anything to do with him, the mother is furious at the invasion and the kittens are thoroughly disturbed.

The owner of a cat sanctuary, where the thirty or so resident cats have been neutered, tells me that when weaned kittens arrive needing a new home, it is the males who play tirelessly with them, and, when they are all exhausted, even curling up with the kittens and soothing them with gentle licking. The female residents, on the other hand, hiss, spit and strike out if the kittens approach. It may be that females have some natural resistance to 'mothering' when their maternal instincts have not been aroused by pregnancy and milk production, while males look on kittens not as needy youngsters but as nonthreatening playmates.

Kitten pool

Among feral cats, who need to find food and defend themselves against predators, several mothers will pool their kittens, and up to forty kittens will live together in one special area. Each mother will feed, wash and shepherd any of the kittens, without giving preference to her own brood, it is quite normal to see a group of kittens, from one to four weeks old all suckling together. This is a matter of survival, so that some of the females are free to go hunting while others play nursemaid and take their turn as hunters later.

Another survival technique, essential to the wild cat, has been programmed so deeply into the cat's make-up, that domestic cats still follow the pattern set by their savage ancestors. In the forest or jungle, a cat would move her kittens to a new nest a couple of days after the birth, then again about four weeks later. She makes the first move because she senses that there is danger in remaining in the same place for too long, as the smells left from the birth could attract predators to the nest. The second move happens when the kittens are ready for weaning. The first two homes would have been chosen for their safety; the next needs to close to the best hunting area, as every time the mother has to leave her litter to find food, the kittens are left defenceless. None of this is necessary for the cherished house cat, provided with regular meals and well protected from danger, but she may well move her kittens anyway. One by one, she takes them by the scruff of the neck and immediately the kitten goes limp, its tail curled upwards between its bent hind legs to minimize the chances of bumping on the ground. When she reaches the chosen spot, the mother opens her jaws and drops the kitten, then goes back for the next one. As she cannot count, she always goes back to the empty nest after the last kitten has been moved, just to check that none have been left behind.

The protective instinct is very strong and mother cats are known for their fierce defence of their infants, if necessary squaring up to predators they would normally make great efforts to avoid and staying steadfast in the face of danger. On the wall of one of Britain's churches, St Augustine's in London, is the record of a devoted feline mother called Faith.

FACING PAGE: *At four weeks old, a kitten can walk quite competently and groom itself.*

ABOVE: *In their first few months of life, kittens are kept busy exploring new sights, scents and textures.*

During the Second World War Faith lived at the vicarage, where she and her kitten slept in a cosy basket in a bedroom. One day in 1940 she carried her kitten down three flights of stairs and set up a new nest in a wall niche where sheet music was normally kept. Though the vicar moved the little family back upstairs three times, Faith always carried the kitten down again and put it back in the wall niche and, in the end, the vicar allowed her to stay. Three nights later a bomb fell on the vicarage and if Faith and her kitten had been upstairs, they would have been killed. As it was, Faith shielded the kitten with her body inside the niche as fire raged, floors fell in and blazing beams fell all around her. Faith never moved and in the morning she and her kitten were both rescued, frightened but without a singed whisker.

Gaining confidence

In the first few days after their birth, the kittens have little awareness of the world about them. If they are lifted out of the kittening box they will begin to cry, but if they are put in a warm, cosy place they will soon settle down to sleep. After a week or so, they are able to distinguish their nest from any other place and will only settle once they are 'home'. Newborn kittens have no way of regulating their own temperature, and if their mother is absent they will all huddle together to keep warm but when they are three weeks old they begin to develop some measure of temperature control. At much the same time, they will start tottering on unsteady legs and begin climbing out of the nesting box to explore.

At four weeks old, they can walk quite competently, their hearing is well developed, and they are learning to groom themselves and are eager to play. The merry, outgoing kitten will be hurling itself into the middle of every scrum, while the shy, retiring kitten is always left on the sidelines. Sometimes there is even a pushy little bully, determined to claim the best of everything for itself. The inquisitive, extrovert kitten will probably make the most suitable pet, particularly in a household with dogs and children, but a hesitant kitten can be very endearing and, though it will need extra patience and coaxing to develop its potential, its relationship with a gentle owner can be most rewarding.

The kitten's experience of both the animal and human world between the ages of two and seven weeks is crucial to its behaviour for the rest of its life. If an orphan is hand-reared, it will have so little experience of its fellows that it may grow up suspicious of other cats and, even if it is not neutered, it may never breed. It never has the opportunity to build up confidence through a normal rough and tumble upbringing within the litter, so even as an adult it remains unsure and hesitant in its relations with the outside world. But, if too much handling in early kittenhood creates problems, too little is just as harmful. Kittens handled regularly before they reach two months old are more playful, more inquisitive and quicker at learning than those left entirely with feline companions. They are also more likely to grow into affectionate, well-adapted cats, more trusting and receptive to their special humans. My parents once owned a cat called Bimbo, whose white Persian

RIGHT: *The kitten's biggest step towards independence is weaning.*

mother had mated with a one-eyed bruiser of a feral tom. The resulting kittens were very beautiful but the owner was so appalled by the unplanned pregnancy that she could never bring herself to touch any of them. In our home Bimbo soon discovered the delights of lap-cuddling but could turn in an instant from a purring softie to a savage attacker as he seized a stroking hand in his teeth, closed in all four sets of claws and raked fiercely with his back feet, leaving bloody scratches from wrist to elbow. His social veneer was only skin deep and his wild ancestry would reassert itself.

Learning from mother

Kittens learn all sorts of skills, from washing themselves to using the litter tray, by watching their mother. If the mother can open door latches or knows how to get extra titbits by begging in a particular way, then as soon as the kittens are old enough they will be copying her. Experi-

LEFT: *Kittens acquire all the important skills in life, from feeding to washing, by copying their mother.*

ments have shown that kittens do not learn nearly so fast or so well if they watch another cat, rather than their mother, performing the same tasks. The mother communicates with them by a series of different sounds, encouraging, reproving, comforting or warning. When in trouble kittens have a distinctive distress call to which all mothers will respond with a gentle 'brrrp', the feline equivalent of 'hush, hush, mother's here'. She will use strong-arm tactics if necessary, cuffing them with a soft paw if they get out of line or taking them by the scruff of the neck and carrying them (or dragging them if they are too heavy to lift) back to the nest.

A free-roaming mother cat will start introducing her kittens to the idea of prey when they are a few weeks old, bringing home a dead bird or mouse so that they can get used to the smell and get the feel of batting it around a little. Later she will bring back live prey and stand guard to see that it does not escape while they practice pouncing and grabbing. Early conditioning will have a great influence on what the grown cat regards as prey. Cats raised with mice as companions will not grow up to be mousers; the

early proximity has wiped out the instinct to regard the mouse as natural prey. Cats brought up with chickens have been known to dive through the middle of a group of baby chicks, any of which would have made an easy catch, to pounce on a hapless sparrow that is trying to steal their food.

Time for play

Kittens begin playing at about three weeks old, usually patting at a moving object like their mother's tail, then discovering that they can move things themselves by batting and poking at them. Soon they are playing with one another, usually two kittens together at first, pawing at one another or rolling over and over together. They have only short bursts of energy and one minute they are playing energetically, the next they are fast asleep, their limbs intertwined. The amount of playing increases at just about the time the wild mother would have to leave her litter for longer periods to hunt for food. After about six weeks the mother is noticeably less tolerant with her kittens, swiping out irritably at them if they hang round her too much. They are

25

no longer 'mummy's babies' and are preparing for independence. When they begin to climb, a whole new world of fun and mischief opens up. One breeder made the mistake of having her sitting room wall redecorated with an embossed paper shortly before the arrival of three litters, with four kittens apiece. As their climbing skills developed, they found just enough toe-hold for their tiny bodies and scampered gaily up the paper, only to get stuck halfway, so that she had to go round the room picking them off, like little bugs. Curtains make another favourite climbing rope, and stories of kittens that make a habit of running up one side of the curtains to sit on the pelmet, keeping it up until they are so big and heavy that the whole lot falls down, are too numerous to mention.

By six weeks it is already hard to tell whether fights between kittens are wholly in fun or rather more serious. By now they can run about and groom themselves efficiently and their vision is excellent. Their eyes are still blue, the birth colour for all kittens, but at about three months this will change and then there is an enormous variety of colouring in the irises. Cats' eyes can be orange, gold, amber, copper, blue, green, hazel, emerald, aquamarine – and all sorts of intermediate shades. Some colours are associated with particular coats: black or blue cats usually have gold, orange or copper eyes; ginger or tortoiseshell cats also tend to gold or copper, silver tabbies to green or hazel, while the sparkling silver chinchilla coat usually goes with green or greeny-blue. Most oriental cats have green eyes, though they may be amber, and white cats sometimes have blue, sometimes orange or copper eyes – and occasionally one of each.

Big step

The biggest single step towards independence is weaning. At first, kittens will put on something like their birth weight every week, and careful breeders will know by weighing them if they are all feeding properly. In the first fortnight after birth it is the mother that decides on feeding times and gathers in her brood but from then onwards the kittens begin to ask for food, though feeding is still very much a communal activity. If one kitten begins to suck, purring its satisfaction, this is a signal to all the others to

FACING PAGE: *Two kittens may be engaged in mock battle one moment, and fast asleep the next.*

line up at the same time. By about five weeks, it no longer matters to the kittens which teat they use to nurse, probably because they now feed as the whim takes them rather than as a group, but by now their teeth are coming through and they are showing an interest in their mother's food, though they are just as likely to walk through it as eat it. Though weaning is a natural process, which would happen without human intervention in the wild, it is not always as straightforward as it sounds. Milly, Billy and Wally were rescued at three days old from a shoe box without airholes, in which they had been left to die. They were bottle fed and when it was time to try solids, Billy and Wally had no trouble at all. Milly was a different story: her owner tried every cereal and baby food known to man but Milly seemed unable or unwilling to lap. Just as she was becoming convinced there was something physiologically wrong with Milly, her owner tipped a little of her daughter's banana milkshake into a saucer and, in an instant, Milly was lapping like a veteran. She has had a passion for bananas ever since and will tear a bunch to pieces in minutes.

All the kittens in a litter will not necessarily begin to eat solids at the same time and, in any case, they will sometimes find it easier, and much more comfortable, to snuggle up to mother for a soothing suck than to set about chewing food. The kittens' emerging teeth can be quite painful for the mother and she may begin to push away her offspring when they try to nurse; though weaning should be complete by eight weeks, some kittens will still continue suckling, regardless of the decreasing milk supply. Kittens taken from their mother too early – and sometimes those that are not – may take to sucking woollen blankets or sweaters, especially those impregnated with the smell of their owners. The blanket fibres can cause problems if they are swallowed. Most grow out of it, but some get quite obsessive and will only eat a meal if there is a blanket alongside, so that they can nibble it as a side dish.

Non-pedigree cats will be ready to leave their mothers at about eight weeks old, pedigrees develop a little more slowly and will usually need ten weeks before they are ready for the outside world. The kittens still have plenty to learn but they will now learn from experience, at a slower rate.

RIGHT: *Kittens are often convinced that their sibling has something much more tasty in their bowl.*

CHAPTER THREE

The Big World

In the wild, kittens would stay with their mother much longer than ten weeks, though she would be denying them access to her milk supply soon after that time. Once they reached sexual maturity they would have to move on and make their own way in the world, and, even among domestic cats, this is recognized as the natural way. Owners quite often allow their pedigree female cat to have one litter before having her spayed, so that they can keep a good quality kitten, but unless there is already a whole family of cats, it can set up long-standing resentment. Ramilla, a friend's loving, gentle Burmese, changed character completely when one of her own kittens joined the household permanently. She became distant and aloof, preferring her bed to a

FACING PAGE: Nothing can stop a young cat from exploring the boundaries of its domain.

lap and avoiding a stroking hand.

Kittens are naturally playful and inquisitive, so most of them adapt very quickly to their new home, where there is plenty to explore and a new family to make them feel the centre of attention, but there are exceptions. When I brought home my two cats, Oliver and Emma, at ten weeks old, Oliver danced about in excitement, ate heartily and set the seal of approval on his new home by falling asleep on my husband's lap. Emma seemed to think that cat butchery could be the only reason for the unwanted move and went into hiding, refusing to eat for twenty-four hours, and for days afterwards only coming out for a quick few mouthfuls at mealtimes. For the first three weeks I was only allowed to stroke her if she was tucked in behind Oliver, so that I had to reach over his body. Later she was to develop into a very affectionate, demanding cat and it is hard to find time for the amount of cuddling she says she needs.

As the kitten's confidence increases, it will get into all sorts of scrapes, and every owner has a story about their particular mischief-maker. There was Shandy, who climbed up the sheets every washday and balanced on the washing line like a tightrope walker, and Smudge, who went missing for half a day and was found fast asleep in the rubbish bin, after diving through the swing top and finding he could not climb out again. Columbo was stuck 27 m (90 ft) up in a conifer tree for two days because early attempts at rescue had only made him climb higher. Neighbours turned out with baking tins and wooden spoons to drive off the crows, who were taking an unhealthy interest in Columbo, before he was finally brought down.

Lasting habits

The kitten is still at an impressionable age and habits set up now will probably last a lifetime. Most indoor cats, trained to use the litter tray by their mothers in infancy, would rather burst than break the habit, so Bosley's owners were horrified when he began ignoring his tray and using their shoes instead. Only after days of trauma did they remember that the last time he used his tray, a loaf of bread had fallen on his head. They thought it quite amusing at the time but to Bosley the tray became a place of danger where missiles would rain down. The tray was moved, to the lasting relief of both cat and owners.

Small children with kittens may make a pretty picture but it is not the best combination in the world: the relationship works better with children who are old enough to treat the kitten as a playmate, rather than a toy. Cats are much more private animals than dogs and they need their own space; even kittens are not always ready for a game. Plenty of rest is essential for their well-being and too much excitement only leads to tummy upsets. For an older child, owning a kitten can develop a real sense of responsibility, as well as a lasting bond of affection. One eight-year-old in our neighbourhood made the kitten a bed in her dolls pram and put it outside for a nap in

RIGHT: *Older children can develop lasting bonds with a kitten, as they both grow up together.*

ABOVE: *Even though it has the size advantage, a dog will often approach a kitten very warily indeed.*

the sunshine every afternoon, just as though she was looking after a baby. When her grandmother decided to take her on a shopping expedition, the pram went too, complete with kitten. It was only when a shop assistant dangled a strip of smoked salmon over the pram that grandmother realised that they were taking a kitten, not a doll, for a ride.

A cat already in residence will probably tolerate a new kitten more readily than another adult cat but that doesn't mean that the established cat will be pleased by the new arrival. Kittens are very lively and can plague a sedate senior beyond endurance, so the new arrival is likely to be attacked a number of times before it learns its place.

Introductions between cats and dogs need to be carefully managed; but as long as the dog is restrained so that the instincts of pursuer and pursued are not aroused, the cat will not take flight, and they can take stock of one another. The dog is often thoroughly bewildered by this little ball of fluff, and its instinct is to sniff at it. When a pawful of needle-like claws lands on its nose, the dog learns to give the kitten a wide berth.

Though in most cases pet rabbits or

hamsters are best kept well away from the cat, some strange friendships have been formed, both inside and out. When twelve-week-old Happy went off to explore the outside world for the first time and disappeared, her owners were out for hours, calling and tapping her food bowl without success. It was only when darkness fell and the security lights went on that they lit up several pairs of eyes. One pair of eyes belonged to Happy, while the others belonged to some young foxes, and now, two years later, Happy still goes out every evening to play with them.

Kittens have very small stomachs but need more food, relative to their size, than mature cats, so they eat four meals a day at ten weeks, then three slightly larger helpings at four months. They often eat until their sides bulge but they know best how much food they need and will walk away when they have had enough. Most cats regulate their food intake efficiently, but there are exceptions. According to the *Guinness Book of Records* the heaviest cat on record was an Australian called Himmy, who weighed in at 23.3 kg (46 lb).

In my experience, some cats are nat-

ABOVE: *Rabbits and cats are not usually a good combination, but this kitten may be young enough to accept a new friend.*

ural thieves and scavengers, always ready to raid the garbage or snatch the food from the plates of other cats in the neighbourhood, and some are not. In cared-for pet cats this bears no relation to the amount they are fed; it is the natural instinct for opportunistic feeding asserting itself.

Cat and mouse

The soft canned food we feed our pets bears little relation to their natural prey, though it contains all the vitamins and minerals necessary for a balanced diet. As opportunists, cats in the wild prey on whatever is available. In European countries this is most likely to be rabbits, birds and rodents but in Australia they add possums and snakes to the menu. Cats eat their catch, bones and all, though they often pluck the indigestible feathers from birds first. Well-fed domestic cats have no need to hunt for food but this in no way dampens their hunting ardour. From early kittenhood they have practised their technique, hiding to wait in patient ambush for siblings, just as they will sit beside a mouse hole watching for the occupant to emerge, and, stalking and pouncing on anything that moves, in the same was that they will eventually stalk a bird. A pet cat will hunt a fly, a spider or a moth with the same dedication that its wild cousin hunts a tasty meal.

A hungry wild cat will kill and eat its prey immediately but domestic cats are more likely to play games, throwing their catch in the air, batting it along the ground with their paws or releasing it for a moment, only to pounce the moment it moves again. The cat may be using every method to prolong the thrill of the chase, for it has enormous pent-up energy and sometimes capers around the prey, leaping high into the air in its excitement. On the other hand, this could be due to inefficiency. Skilled hunters kill their prey with a single, swift bite, but cats whose mothers had no opportunity to hunt, or those that hunt for fun rather than for food, may not have the proper training to master the killing bite. Though throwing the catch in the air can be useful in the case of a large rodent, to stun and disorientate it and make it easier to handle, the domestic cat over-reacts and gives the same treatment to a tiny mouse. When it lifts a paw and allow the victim to make an abortive dash for freedom, it may

FACING PAGE: *It is hard to believe that behind such innocent faces lurk the souls of born pilferers!*

simply be checking to see if it is dead. In most cases the prey is never killed; instead it dies of shock or injury. All the apparent cruelty of the 'cat and mouse' games may come about because, once the cat has made its catch, it simply doesn't know what to do with it.

This uncertainty may be the reason that owners often receive unwanted gifts from their cats: dead birds in the sink, a headless rat in the armchair or mangled voles laid out on the dining table. Some experts think that the cats are simply contributing to the family food supply or trying to teach us the rudiments of hunting, as their mothers once taught them. Whatever the reason, it is little comfort to the owner that has to fish a corpse from his shoe every morning.

Establishing a territory

Every cat needs its own territory. This is yet another instinct programmed into the cat, so that territorial behaviour persists even though, with a pet animal, the need to keep rivals away from its food supplies no longer exists. The extent of the territory depends on the surroundings and the status of the cat, with entire toms con-

trolling as much as ten times the ground belonging to a female. Indoor cats may set up a favourite seat or a spot on the bed as their territory and drive off any other cat that tries to encroach. My cats live indoors where Oliver 'owns' a particular armchair and Emma a bean bag, and this is obviously understood between them. Oliver will occasionally use the bean bag, just to show that he could if he wanted, but he never looks completely comfortable. Emma sits in the armchair once in a while, but jumps off smartly if Oliver heads her way.

Within a litter of kittens, competition shows itself early and, as they mature, this turns into the territorial drive. When a kitten arrives in its new home, it may be nervous of going far beyond its back door because it may be encroaching on another cat's established territory. At first it will be most confident when it can accompany a member of the family that is weeding the path or mowing the lawn, but in time it will carve out its own patch and defend it against all comers. This rarely means fighting, for cats have all sorts of strategies for avoiding full-scale confrontation.

Cats mark the boundaries of their terri-

RIGHT: *Like children, kittens can have a habit of comfort sucking – blankets and hair are prime targets.*

tory in several ways. They rub their faces against walls, posts and trees, leaving behind the scent from sebaceous glands on their heads; they leave visual signals by scratching, also leaving behind scent from the sweat on their paws. Toms in particular spray hedges and bushes leaving a pungent odour; both neutered males and females may also spray, but without leaving the smell humans find offensive. These markers will tell other cats how recently the territory owner has passed, so they need to be renewed fre-quently. Most cats check their territory several times a day; this explains why cats beg to go out, only to cry to come in again almost immediately. Indoor cats, secure in undisputed territory, will not need to spray. When a cat does spray indoors it is probably because there are several cats in the household and they are trying to claim their own space, or because a cat flap has been fitted, so that outdoor and indoors are no longer clearly defined and the cat feels that it has to demonstrate its ownership to any intruder.

CHAPTER FOUR

Bodywork

When a kitten is born its eyes are closed and its ears folded back, but its senses of touch and smell are already well developed. It finds its mother by the warmth coming from her body, guided by its nose leather, which it uses as a thermometer. The nose is the part of the cat's body most sensitive to heat and cold and all through its life it will use its nose to test the temperature of its food, so that it never risks burning its mouth. The kitten's first sensual pleasure will come from touch, as the mother licks it immediately after birth; in the first weeks she will spend a good deal of time grooming her offspring. Stroking our pet cats is the nearest we come to a mother's licking and it brings back all the pleasurable sensations of its earliest days.

FACING PAGE: Stalking an insect in the long grass, this kitten shows that it has already taken its first lessons as a hunter.

The new kitten will locate the mother's teat by smell and return to the same one at every feed. In cats, smell and taste are so closely linked that if a tiny kitten has a respiratory illness, it may not be able to suckle. Once it is weaned, the kitten will always sniff food before deciding to take a mouthful. Cat food manufacturers are well aware of the importance of smell and a newly opened can may scent the whole house, but a cat can detect immediately if food is past its best, long before a human knows that it is 'off'. When it is small a kitten will 'test' any unfamiliar object by licking it. As it matures it uses its nose to investigate strangers, whether people or cats, as well as new places or objects.

The cat has a special sensory organ in the roof of its mouth, which gives it the

unique ability to analyse particular scents. If a cat stops dead in its tracks and seems to sneer, opening its mouth slightly and curling back its lip, then it is 'flehming': drawing in an odour and passing it across this organ.

Developing senses

The kitten's ears will take up to three weeks to become erect, when it can then begin to distinguish sounds but it will be some weeks before they develop their adult sensitivity. When they do, the results are impressive: a cat can hear a range of ten octaves, two more than humans, and it can detect the faintest squeak or rustle of its prey.

Vision, too, takes a while to develop and it is three weeks before the kittens can identify their mother by sight rather than smell or touch. The cat's eyes are those of the nocturnal hunter, with pupils that dilate and contract according to the amount of light available. When the light

LEFT: *A kitten explores as much by smell and touch as by sight.*

is dim, they cover almost the whole circle of the eye, to make the most of the slightest glimmer. Though cats cannot see in the dark, they need only about one sixth of the light humans require because of the layer of cells at the back of the retina, which can reflect and amplify any light. This is the reason that cats' eyes glow in the dark, which in the superstitious Middle Ages led to the belief that they had evil supernatural powers. Though cats can distinguish colours, this is not a highly developed ability because it is of little use to a creature that hunts at night, when all its prey looks grey or black.

Vital equipment

Whiskers and claws, both vital equipment for the cat, are present at birth. The claws, which are held in recessive sheaths between the pads, grow continuously, like human fingernails, and indoor cats, who do not have the opportunity to wear them down naturally, will need a regular trim. Special muscles enable the cat to extend and retract the claws, which are essential for climbing and gripping prey, as well as in defence or attack. In some countries, including the USA, cats are regularly de-clawed to prevent them from ruining furniture; an operation that involves removing the cells at the base of the claw and part of the bone as well, so that the claws will not grow again. In other countries, including Britain, this is only allowed for medical reasons, as it leaves the cat defenceless.

The whiskers are stiff hairs embedded in bunches of nerves that transmit messages to the brain, so they are very sensitive to touch and to the change in air

ABOVE: *The kitten as hunter: its gaze is unblinking, its haunches tensed to spring and its tail twitches in anticipation.*

43

currents, which conveys the message that there are obstacles in its path. They tell the cat if the gap ahead is wide enough to take its body, even when it is too dark to see, and help it to locate the right spot for the bite that will kill its prey.

Rest and action

By the time it is six weeks old, the kitten will have developed adult sleeping patterns and it will spend 75 per cent of its adult life sleeping. It is most lively at dawn and dusk and sleeps most in the middle of both day and night. The majority of the time it is napping, a shallow sleep where its temperature drops a little, its blood pressure remains steady and its muscles are still slightly tensed. Then, for six or seven minutes at a time, it will fall into a deeper sleep. It is during the periods of deep sleep that the cat dreams, its paws and whiskers twitching as it makes little sounds of excitement or fear, but electroencephalogram (EEG) readings

LEFT: *It's just as well a kitten starts with nine lives; this one seems set to use up several before it grows up.*

show that the cat's brain patterns vary little between sleeping and waking; it is always alert for the slightest unusual sound and ready to spring into action in an instant. Thus the cat makes sure that no one will catch it unawares.

When it arrives in its new home the kitten can run and leap, grab and pounce, but it still has to develop its strength and co-ordination, learn to estimate jumps, and test out its sense of balance. Eventually it will be able to leap five times its own height, balance on narrow surfaces like a tightrope walker, and extricate itself from seemingly impossible positions, but all these skills need practice. One new owner was unaware of the attraction that her 2.5 m (8 ft) Christmas tree had for her fourteen-week-old kitten George until she heard a bang-tinkle-crash sound from the living room and hurried in to see her kitten sliding down from the top of the tree in slow motion, clinging for dear life to the Christmas angel and scattering baubles as he came. He had scaled the tree in a moment of excitement but was too inexperienced to find any way of getting down. Descending after a climb is, in fact, one of the manoeuvres the cat finds most difficult;

ABOVE: *Much growling and hissing may accompany feeding time, with each young cat having an insatiable curiosity about its neighbour's food.*

45

kittens may not have the confidence to attempt it, so if they are allowed outside, they often get stuck in trees. Though they ascend easily by means of their claws and the powerful muscles of their hindquarters, neither of these help as they come down, so they have to shuffle backwards until they are within reach of the ground and can jump down.

Kittens frequently get into scrapes because of their love of climbing but fortunately they seldom hurt themselves. One of the reasons that cats have the reputation for having nine lives is the 'self-righting reflex', which is present from birth. This is due to a special apparatus in the inner ear that tells the brain the exact position and rate of movement of the head and enables it to send instant messages for the body to right itself. It works like this: first the head turns until it is upright, then the front paws come up towards the head to protect the chin. The spine twists until it is in line with the head and with every movement, the tail is used as a counterbalance. Just before touchdown, all four limbs stretch out as the cat arches its back to spread the force of the impact throughout its body. Hence the belief that cats always land on their feet

but, though cats have walked away from twenty-storey falls, this is not always the case and every year numbers of injured cats need veterinary care.

The maturing predator

The first teeth can just be seen inside the gums of the new-born kitten and within six weeks they are strong and sharp as small needles. These will serve the kitten for four or six months, then they fall out as the permanent teeth come through. The process is usually so trouble-free that owners are not aware that it is happening. The full set is made up of four canines, twelve incisors, ten premolars and four molars. They are designed for biting, tearing and shearing, but not for chewing, so the cat's food must be chopped into pieces small enough to swallow, or it must be big enough to allow the cat to tear out chunks, as it would with its natural prey.

At six months the kitten that goes outdoors will be ready to hunt. Good technique is fascinating to watch. The cat first sits up very straight, its head turning slowly to measure the exact position of the prey, its ears erect to take in every

FACING PAGE: *A ten-week-old tabby is just about to learn that it cannot walk on water.*

LEFT: *This kitten is not just sniffing some sweet-smelling flowers; it can detect the scent of other animals on the grass.*

FACING PAGE: *The adult cat is both a controlled predator and a civilized and elegant companion.*

sound. It then drops down, crouching on all fours and creeps cautiously along. It will crawl a little way, then go into a short sprint. It freezes for a few moments in case the movement has alerted the prey, then begins stalking again. When it gets near enough to ambush its victim, it drops low in the grass or behind a bush and gathers itself for the final onslaught, every muscle tense. Then it suddenly shoots forward, lifts its front paws from the ground and pounces. An efficient hunter will pin down the prey with its front paws as it lands; a less experienced cat may have to make several snatches. It will use its front paws to turn the prey into the right position for the death bite or it may roll over onto its side, raking at the victim with its back claws and then biting.

As the kitten matures it is easy to see why the cat has been such a successful animal, flourishing in most parts of the world. It has the strength and the concentration of the ruthless killer, the agility of an athlete and the grace of the natural aristocrat. It is expert at conserving its energy but capable of sharp bursts of speed, which can be triggered in an instant.

49

CHAPTER FIVE

Kitten Talk

As it grows up, the kitten will form a close bond with its special humans, often following them around, waiting at the door to greet them when they arrive home, bedding down on their laps, sensing their moods and even pining when they are separated for any length of time. This is a much closer relationship than they would ever form with another animal. Even in feral cat colonies, where cats live together for mutual advantage, they may sit close together but they seldom touch and though two cats may hunt within sight of one another, they do not join forces.

Cats probably see us as the ideal companions, non-competitive and non-aggressive, ready playmates, providers of warmth and security and food. Some say that food is the key to it all with cats, ever

opportunists, humouring us because they know it is to their advantage, but this does not explain why cats often choose, as their favourite human, a member of the family that never feeds them. Another theory is that, because they never have to forge an independent lifestyle, they regard us as substitute mothers and keep their kittenish behaviour, playing and cuddling and following their 'mother' all their lives.

When only a few days old kittens can be heard purring as they suckle, though at this age they do not respond to a stroking hand by purring. It is simply a sign of contentment to tell their mother that all is well; later they send the same happy signal to their owners. When they lie purring on our laps, cats also knead with

FACING PAGE: *With proper attention a shy kitten can become a gentle and devoted pet.*

51

their paws, squeezing their claws in and out, just as they used to knead their mother's abdomen to stimulate the milk supply. Obviously the pleasure of settling down on something soft and warm brings back beautiful memories, for they will act the same way with anything treadable. By the time a kitten is a month old, it will be asking its mother for milk or attention by rubbing its arched body against her, its tail straight in the air. Every owner later recognizes this as 'cupboard love'.

Staying playful

Wild cats will play together when young but as they mature and face up to the realities of life, of finding enough food and protecting themselves from predators, they abandon this behaviour. Pet cats will go on playing, in varying degrees, throughout their lives. Early play helps the kitten to learn about its environment and its relation with others, and follows a set pattern of development. First comes the rough and tumble with their littermates, with much rolling on their backs. This turns into wrestling when they grasp a playmate with their front paws and kick with their hind legs. At about five weeks old, they play more frequently and in larger groups and further away from their mother. They now learn to pounce and practise mock threats, arching their backs and turning sideways on their playmates to make themselves look as fearsome as possible, just as they will do later when trying to dispatch an intruder from their territory. Soon they are leaping and chasing, playing hide and seek round the furniture. Males are always more interested in playing with objects than females, but both sexes will be batting at pencils or tossing balls of wool. It is noticeable that if they have the choice their favourite toys will be shaped like their natural prey. When pet shops sell cloth mice, they are appealing to the cat's natural preferences. By the time kittens are fully weaned, their play is more purposeful: now they carry the cloth mice about clamped in their teeth and climb on the backs of their littermates, getting the feel of the neckbite that will one day mean death to their captured prey.

From about three months the kittens become more interested in exploring and watching the world go by and gambol about a bit less; but it is at about five months when, in the wild, the litter would

FACING PAGE: *On a farm, there are endless games for three lively kittens to play.*

ABOVE: *A vivacious kitten watches her sisters from her hiding place in the straw, ready to dash out and surprise them.*

FACING PAGE: *At five or six weeks of age, kittens play more frequently and roam further from their mother.*

fluffy toy from below as they would scoop a fish from the water and they swat at anything dangled before them on a piece of string or elastic as they might swat at a bird they have failed to pin down. Every cat will find its own favourite game: I know one that retrieves bits of crumpled paper and lays them at his owner's feet for a repeat performance, and another that takes wrapped sweets from the sweet bowl and plays football with them down the stairs.

Cat communication

The more you talk to your kitten the more likely it is to respond. Many cats come to answer back readily and their owners can tell, from the tone of the meow, whether the cat's mood is contented, demanding or frustrated. Owners often find that their cats try to join in a telephone conversation and think the cat is simply trying to claim their attention but it is much more likely that when the cat hears you talking when there is no one else in the room, it assumes that it is being addressed and comes across to respond.

disperse and the young cats are beginning to feel sexual urges, that the amount of time spent playing declines dramatically. All the same, domestic cats with indulgent owners keep their love of play, and regular play sessions are essential for the well-being of indoor cats. Most games mimic natural hunting behaviour: cats pounce on a moving string just as they would pounce on a mouse, they scoop a

One of the most appealing messages

the cat can give is the 'silent meow', when it gazes wistfully up at you and opens its mouth but no sound comes out. This may originate in the ultrasonic cry given by kittens when they first become mobile and begin to explore the nest. It is inaudible to humans but the mother cat responds. Perhaps the silent meow is not really silent at all.

The cat has plenty of other signals, besides its voice, to show its intentions and needs. It shows nerves by twitching its ears and licking its lips. A straight tail is a friendly sign; a tail held low and slightly bent is threatening. The ears of a relaxed and peaceful cat will be held upwards but slightly sideways; once it is alerted they shoot up and point forwards in concentration. Eyes not only respond to light but to moods: when the cat is angry, wary or excited, the pupils will be large and black; when it is relaxed and contented, the pupils will contract to narrow, vertical slits. For a cat, staring can be a sign of aggression – two cats engaged in a dispute will glare fixedly at one another, each trying to make the other back down. If eye contact is broken for some reason, they may both give up the idea of a fight and edge away from one another. Animal behaviour experts say that a cat that, confronted by a group of strangers, unerringly picks the lap of the only cat hater, is simply choosing the least threatening, because the cat hater is the only one not gazing at it. On the other hand, our cats are great people watchers and they stare at us quite a lot. Staring back seems quite acceptable within a relaxed relationship and cats will often respond with a long, slow blink, a friendly greeting that shows all is well with their world.

Friendly cats will wash one another, as a companionable or soothing gesture, and sometimes when they are relaxed and happy on a lap, they will wash their human friends, their rasping tongues gently sandpapering our hands. Though they groom first and foremost to keep themselves clean – and most cats are fanatical about cleanliness – they will also set about washing themselves if they are trying to pretend they are unconcerned about what is going on or if they are not quite sure what to do next in a particular situation. If they fall off the television set when they have been trying to catch a bird flying across the screen, or go skidding across the table on some papers,

RIGHT: *With ears pricked forward and eyes keen but not dilated, this kitten is clearly feeling intrigued but unthreatened.*

ABOVE: *An open drawer or cupboard may be appropriated as a kitten's favourite hiding place.*

Whether it lives indoors or outdoors, it will probably move round its favourite sitting and sleeping places at roughly the same time each day. It will have its regular playtime and nap time. Pet cats have little control over the major happenings in their lives and they get their security from their routines, from the fact that meals come at the same time every day and that the things around them are thoroughly impregnated with their own scent. For some cats, even the arrival of a new piece of furniture can be unsettling and can cause a temporary character change. They become very attached to places, and if they are uprooted they sometimes react with total panic. Branded on my memory is a house move my family made when I was a teenager and my cat, Panda, was five months old. We did everything we could to make it easy on him, confining him to a room where he would not be disturbed, but he went berserk, hurling himself against the windows and door and screaming his distress. I just managed to catch him before he dived up the chimney, regardless of the fire blazing in the hearth. In the end he crawled under my skirt as I sat on the floor. Any movement started him wailing

they will begin a quick grooming session: perhaps to cover their embarrassment or to calm themselves after a fright. Cat lovers are sometimes quite hurt to find that when they have petted a cat, it immediately begins washing, as though to remove the human touch, but it is probably because it is tasting the scent left on its coat by our hands.

Daily routine

Once settled with its new family, the kitten will soon set its daily routine.

RIGHT: *A cat may groom itself simply when it is feeling relaxed and comfortable – not always for hygiene reasons.*

again so we both crouched there for the rest of the day.

Cats often seem to have an uncanny ability to sense what is about to happen. They predict when they are about to go on a car journey, when the family is going off on holiday, and when a new baby is expected, and react by going into hiding, becoming sulky and distant or showing signs of insecurity or possessiveness. Owners who insist that they 'couldn't pos-

sibly have known' put it all down to extra sensory perception, but it is more likely that the cat senses the slightest change in the conduct of the household; extra activity or new equipment arriving, or a pregnant woman who walks more heavily and smells different. The appearance of a suitcase or the faintest creak of the cat basket is enough to convey the message and, for the routine-loving cat, it is all bad news.

CHAPTER SIX

Classy Kittens

Though dogs have been bred for centuries, first for special purposes such as hunting or guarding and later for their looks and individual appeal, selective breeding of cats only began about one hundred years ago. So far, the basic cat shape has defied all attempts to change it. A rounder face, smaller ears or slimmer body can be developed, in the way that the nose of the Persian has been shortened and the nose of the Siamese lengthened, but so far efforts to produce 'toy' breeds have been doomed to failure.

A few of today's breeds, like the Havana Brown, are 'designer' cats but most originally came with their main characteristics in-built, and some of the most curious breeds were the result of spontaneous mutations, with the first kittens coming as a complete surprise to their owners. They are then taken up by interested cat fanciers, who improve and refine the most desirable characteristics while trying to eradicate any 'faults'. When breeding a variety from abroad for the first time or trying to replicate an unusual kitten that has cropped up in a litter, it is often necessary to mate a mother and son, a father and daughter, or two litter mates, and this is called 'in-breeding'. Though it has its disadvantages, since the resulting kittens may not be as strong or disease resistant as those more conventionally bred, it may be the only way to carry on a line successfully; the more corresponding genes the two parents have, the more likely they are to pass on the desired characteristics to their offspring.

FACING PAGE: Burmese cats keep their active, playful nature throughout their adult lives.

Basic types

There are two basic body types among cats. One is the stocky shape with a rounded head, round eyes and short sturdy legs; the other is a more elongated creature with a svelte body, long head with almond-shaped eyes, and elegant limbs – but there are, of course, all sorts of variations in between.

Shorthairs were the original alley cats of Britain and Europe, where the prettiest kittens were adopted as household pets, and when the early breeding programmes began in the late nineteenth century, the best specimens were selected to carry on and improve the line. Harrison Weir, who organized the world's first full-scale cat show and drew up the first breed standards, wrote that 'the ordinary garden cat has survived every kind of hardship and persecution. That he exists at all is a tribute to his strength of character and endurance.' The short coat was the natural result of evolution: it was the most useful length for an independent cat being less likely to cause trouble with furballs in the digestive system than long hair.

British and European Shorthairs have small litters, with three kittens as an average, but they are healthy and hardy. They start off as pretty, cuddly kittens but grow into large, sturdy cats - too large sometimes, because they love their food - with deep, broad chests and short legs, rounded faces and big round eyes, so that some people describe them as looking permanently astonished. They come in a wide range of colours, though the final effect will not be seen until the kittens grow up. Blue kittens tend to have tabby markings. Blacks often have a reddish tinge, Creams may be darker in the first few months, and the Tipped varieties (where the tip of the hair is a different colour from the root) often start off with longer coats, which disappear in the adults.

Shared ancestry

American Shorthairs share the same ancestry as British and European Shorthairs, for the first cats went to North America with the early settlers and shared the tough pioneer life. They were such good mousers that they were a welcome addition to any early farming community. Nowadays the kittens are particularly

FACING PAGE: *A Tonkinese and a Balinese kitten play amongst the roses.*

confident and full of courage and grow into adults that are more true to the original type than the British or European varieties, which have been interbred with Persians along the way. They are more lightly built, with narrower faces and thick, hard coats, not as plush as their relatives across the Atlantic. All three types are known as intelligent, affectionate pets with pleasant natures and plenty of energy.

In 1966 in New York State, one kitten in a litter of six farmyard cats stood out because of his unusual coat, which was crinkled and wiry. When he was mated with an ordinary domestic cat, two out of the four resulting kittens had wiry hair; this was the beginning of the American Wirehair, similar in appearance to the Shorthairs, but with a dense, harsh coat, springy to the touch, set off by curly whiskers.

The Egyptian Mau, the only natural breed of spotted cat, probably originated from the street-corner cat of Egypt; the founder of the modern breed was a kitten called Baba, who came from Cairo and was taken to the USA by the Russian Princess Troubetskoy. Mau is the Egyptian word for cat and enthusiasts claim

that the breed is directly descended from the cats of ancient times when they were revered in Egypt for their connection with the cat-headed goddess Bastet, who stood for good luck and prosperity. They have on their foreheads the same 'M' marking that is seen on cat statues preserved from the time of the Pharaohs. Mau kittens, born with obvious spots, are

ABOVE: *This blue Abyssinian kitten affects a proud posture, up on its toes with tail arched.*

FACING PAGE: *A sorrel Abyssinian nuzzles her kitten affectionately.*

lively and playful from the start and grow into strong active cats, who like people.

Breeds from Asia

Another ancient breed of cat is the Japanese Bobtail, known for centuries as the Mi-Ke cat in its home country, where it was much valued in past centuries. Then, in the early seventeenth century, when Japan's important silk industry was being destroyed by the burgeoning rodent population, owners were ordered to turn their cats loose to hunt down the vermin. It was only when American visitors arrived after the Second World War that the cat fanciers among them noticed the unusual cats with their white, black and red colouring and tiny, rabbit-like tails that they wag happily in welcome. They were imported to the USA for their novelty value and soon became established as a recognized breed. Bobtails, still considered good-luck cats in the Far East, are very agile cats, friendly and blessed with a high degree of intelligence. When two Bobtails mate, the kittens will always be Bobtails but if a Bobtail mates with any other type of cat, they will produce kittens with normal tails.

Cats similar to the Russian Blue are still found in the colder regions of Russia, but their Western history began in the 1860s when they were brought to Britain by merchant seamen. At first they were called Archangel Cats, after their port of origin and quickly became popular. 'Ruskies' are graceful cats with long legs and short, plushy coats, blue with a silver sheen. Kittens are born with fluffy coats and sometimes faint tabby markings that disappear as they get older. They are quiet and charming, happy to live indoors where they can entertain themselves for long periods, but they are sometimes quite shy. Black and White Russians are now being bred, particularly in New Zealand, and the Scandinavians have produced a rather darker version of the more familiar Blue.

Rare mutations

Several particularly interesting breeds – the Sphynx, the Scottish Fold and the two types of Rex cats – were the result of rare mutations, with a single 'different' kitten standing out from the litter. In the case of the Sphynx, this was a 'bald' kitten, born to an ordinary black and white domestic

66

RIGHT: *Turkish van cats have a reputation for being one of the few cat breeds that will willingly enter the water.*

cat in Canada in the 1960s. There were earlier reports of other hairless cats, where the parents were Siamese, both in the USA and in France, but the Canadian cat was the founder of the breed. Sphynx kittens are born covered in fine, soft hair but this soon disappears, leaving them with a fine black-coloured down on just the face, paws, ears and the end of the tail. In their first months their skin is heavily wrinkled, as though they were wearing a coat too big for them, but they grow into it in time, leaving wrinkles only around the head. These quiet, friendly cats find stroking uncomfortable, need bathing often and must have protection from the sun, as well as from cold.

A white farm kitten called Susie, born on Tayside in 1961, was the first of the Scottish Folds. When she was born her ears were floppy, just like those of her littermates, but when the ears on the other kittens began to straighten, at two or three weeks, Susie's folded down and forwards. When she produced kittens one of

LEFT: *A tortoiseshell-and-white kitten with the typically sturdy build of the British shorthair.*

them, Snooks, took after her and was adopted by breeders. They soon found that when two Folds were mated the kittens were likely to develop abnormalities in the hindquarters, so they are usually mated to straight-eared cats. In Britain Folds were banned from competition in the 1970s because of worries that it would be impossible to keep their ears clean, but they were exported to the US, where they have been very popular. The round face, wide open eyes and folded ears of this sweet-natured cat give it a rather startled expression, which is very endearing.

The first Cornish Rex kitten was Kallibunker, born in 1950, and the first Devon Rex was Kirlee, born in the neighbouring county, who arrived in 1960. Both had ordinary, straight-coated mothers and littermates but both were born with curly coats and whiskers. At first breeders thought they must be the result of the same gene mutation, but any mating between the Cornish and Devon strains produced only straight-coated kittens. A Rex also appeared in Germany in the 1950s and later matings showed that the German and Cornish Rexes have the same genetic pattern, which differs from that of the Devon.

Rexes are great extroverts and from the first weeks the kittens are forward and full of life, always looking for some new mischief. The Devon Rex has a coarser, thinner coat than the Cornish and is a more delicate looking cat. It has a pixie-like face with large, bat-wing ears make the kittens look as if they might well fly away.

Natural or manufactured

By contrast, the Havana (called Havana Brown in the USA), called after the cigar because of its rich chestnut colour, is a deliberately developed breed, developed from the Siamese in the UK in the early 1950s, and exported to the USA a few years later. The Havana has the elegant body of the Siamese (though the American version is more like the Russian Blue in build) and a slightly wistful look. It is highly intelligent, playful and becomes deeply attached to its owners, so that people matter more than places in its life. The queens call loudly and often, sometimes driving their owners to distraction. The kittens are born the same colour as their parents, though there is usually a scattering of temporary white hairs in

ABOVE: *Sleepy lilac point Siamese kittens cluster for a nap.*

FACING PAGE: *These seven-week-old Burmese kittens will develop darker coat colouring as they mature.*

female that founded the line was imported to the USA from Burma in 1930 but when the early Burmese were first shown, other breeders insisted that they were Siamese with faulty colouring. Feelings ran so high at a major show in San Francisco in 1938 that the cats had to be withdrawn. Since they arrived in the UK in 1948, Burmese have become very popular in show classes.

Burmese make very good mothers and breed easily and abundantly. The kittens have paler coats than the adults. They are very active and playful cats and keep their kittenish love of mischief all their lives.

The royal cats

their coats, but their fur only develops its high gloss when they become adults.

No one is quite sure whether the Burmese is a man-made or a natural breed. Some enthusiasts claim that it was one of the ancient cats of Burma, kept in monasteries and much revered. It seems likely, however, that it came from breeding between Siamese and other types of cats common in the East. The brown

When two Siamese, brought to Britain from the royal court of Siam, were exhibited at the very first cat show, at Crystal Palace in 1885, they created a considerable stir and were denounced as 'unnatural' by lovers of the native cats. However, admiration for their distinctive looks, with the contrast between the coat colour and the darker 'points' – face, ears, paws and tail – grew quickly and they were soon much in demand, both in

Britain and the USA. The early Siamese were less elegant and more cobby in shape than the modern breed and often had squinting eyes and a pronounced kink in the tail. One legend says that when a sacred goblet was stolen from a Buddhist temple in Siam the two temple cats were sent to track it down. When at last it was found, the male cat returned to the temple with the news while the female stayed to guard the treasure. All day she fixed her eyes on the goblet and at night, while she slept, she curled her tail round it for safety. By the time the monks arrived to claim their property, she had a pronounced squint and a permanent bend in her tail, both of which she passed on to her kittens.

Siamese are very easy to breed, reliably producing two large litters a year and the kittens develop quickly, opening their eyes in three or four days and showing their individual personalities right from the start. They are born white and their main coat colour, which will deepen throughout their lives, will only begin to show after a few days while the points may take several weeks to appear. They grow into delicately boned adults, their bodies stronger than they look, with bright blue eyes, extrovert, demanding personalities, and loud voices.

Longhaired arrivals

Persians (officially known as Longhairs in Britain) with their large, brilliant eyes, are cats with enormous 'chocolate box' appeal. Their long-haired ancestors caused quite a stir when they first reached Europe from Asia in the sixteenth century. They came from cold, mountainous regions where the long coat had probably developed by a process of natural selection, as it gave good protection from the elements. The early Persians were apparently fiery little creatures but the modern breed is docile, sweet-tempered and fond of people, so that it makes a good family pet.

At the end of the last century, when Persians had been exhibited in the first cat shows, it was fashionable for the household of every British aristocrat to own a White Persian, and they were much in demand as exports to the USA. Now there is a wide range of colours, bicolours, tabby, tortoiseshell and colourpoint, with the points displaying a different colour from the rest of the coat.

FACING PAGE: *These blue-cream Persians (or Longhairs, as they are known in Britain) would make sweet-natured pets.*

ABOVE: *Chinchillas are beautiful cats; their white coats are tipped with black, brown or red, giving off a silvery sparkle.*

appear in one litter: a Cream father and a Blue mother and will produce Blue males and Blue Cream females, and a Cream mother and Blue father will produce Cream males and Blue-Cream females. Whatever their colour, Persian kittens are playful and cuddly and will stay that way for the rest of their lives.

Ten years of selective breeding in both Britain and the USA produced the Himalayan (or Colourpoint), a cat with Persian looks and coat but Siamese colouring. The kittens are born white and their 'points' colour, which may be choco-late, blue, lilac, orange or tortie, takes several weeks to develop. Their temperament will be a cross between Persian and Siamese; more demanding than the Persian but more docile than the Siamese. Unlike the Persian, the Himalayan makes a good mouser.

Legend says that the Birman, the sacred temple cat of Burma, was once white from head to toe. When invaders from Siam broke into the temple they killed the priest, Mun-Ha, who lay dying beneath the golden statue of the goddess, with her sapphire eyes. The temple cat walked softly over his body and jumped onto the statue, thus transferring the

Kittens do not always show their true colour at first: Whites often start off with pinkish fur, Blacks may look rusty or have a smattering of white hairs, and Tortoise-shells often look so dark it is hard to find any trace of coloured patches. Both Blues and Creams may have tabby markings that fade later. Blues and Creams often

RIGHT: *The Himalayan (or Colourpoint) cat is more inquisitive than the Persian, yet quieter than the Siamese.*

75

priest's soul to the goddess. Immediately the cat's coat became golden white and its eyes sapphire blue. Its face, tail and legs took on the colour of the earth and only its feet, where they had touched the priest, remained white. A more prosaic explanation for the Birman's striking colouring and its long silky hair is that it resulted from a cross between a Siamese and a Bicolour Longhair, long before it left Burma.

Birman kittens are large, healthy and very active, and although they quieten down as they reach adulthood, they remain busy and playful. They are gentle cats, intelligent and fond of following their owners about. Though they are quite well-behaved, they need freedom and don't like to be confined.

Persians were imported to the United States at the turn of the century and the Birmans first arrived in 1959, but the home-grown variety of longhaired American cat is the Maine Coon, so-called because the pioneers thought that it was produced by mating between a cat and a racoon, because of its big bushy tail, but this is biologically impossible. In fact, the Maine Coons were probably the descendants of cats brought from overseas by sailors and merchants, which developed shaggy coats to keep out the winter cold.

They are large, powerful cats with a gentle and affectionate disposition and they make a gentle, chirping sound instead of a full-blown meow. Maine Coon kittens are big and strong, with feet big enough to use as snow shoes and they grow into adults weighing as much as 13.5 kg (30 lb). They are easy to teach, take well to performing tricks and they love to climb trees.

Pedigree puss

Every kitten belonging to a recognized breed should be registered under an individual name when it is just a few weeks old. Its pedigree is its family tree where the names and championship status of the last three or four generations will be recorded. Each country has its own governing body, or bodies, which formally approve the standards for each breed as well as registering pedigrees and sponsoring cat shows. In the UK, the country that pioneered cat showing and breeding since 1910, this has been the Governing Council of the Cat Fancy. The United States has several organizations, the

FACING PAGE: *Birmans have the round eyes and long coat of a Longhair, combined with the distinctive 'points' of a Siamese.*

largest of them being the Cat Fanciers' Association. Australia, too, has a number of bodies, because the cat population is dispersed over such a large area. In continental Europe, organizations in twelve countries belong to the FIFE (Fédération Internationale Feline d'Europe). Breeds accepted by the leading body in one country are not necessarily recognized for competition in another. There is no international consensus on standards and though some breeds are much the same throughout the world, others have developed along different lines in different countries.

Each body has its own set of rules for cat shows and in most classes only registered pedigree cats or kittens will be allowed to compete. There is also a 'provisional' or 'experimental' class for cats with a 'new look' or a different kind of coat. If the new type of cat raises enough interest and can breed true to type for three generations, the owner can hope to have it registered with the governing body as a new breed.

LEFT: *This silver tabby British shorthair kitten may be a show champion of the future.*

Index